School Projects

SURVIVAL GUIDES

Presentations

Barbara A. Somervill

Heinemann
LIBRARY

www.heinemannlibrary.co.uk
Visit our website to find out more information about Heinemann Library books.

To order:
☎ Phone 44 (0) 1865 888066
🖹 Send a fax to 44 (0) 1865 314091
💻 Visit the Heinemann bookshop at www.heinemannlibrary.co.uk to browse our catalogue and order online.

Heinemann Library is an imprint of Capstone Global Library Limited, a company incorporated in England and Wales having its registered office at 7 Pilgrim Street, London, EC4V 6LB – Registered company number: 6695582

Heinemann is a registered trademark of Pearson Education Limited, under licence to Capstone Global Library Limited

Text © Capstone Global Library Limited 2009
First published in hardback in 2009
Paperback edition first published in 2010

Edited by Nancy Dickmann and Kate DeVilliers
Designed by Richard Parker and Hart McLeod
Picture research by Mica Brancic
Production by Victoria Fitzgerald

Originated by Dot Gradations Ltd
Printed in China by Leo Paper Products Ltd

ISBN 978 0 431931 74 6 (hardback)
13 12 11 10 09
10 9 8 7 6 5 4 3 2 1

ISBN 978 0 431931 79 1 (paperback)
14 13 12 11 10
10 9 8 7 6 5 4 3 2 1

British Library Cataloguing in Publication Data
Somervill, Barbara A.
Presentations. – (School projects survival guides)
371.3'7
A full catalogue record for this book is available from the British Library.

Acknowledgements
We would like to thank the following for permission to reproduce photographs:
© Corbis pp. **4** (Charles Gupton), **12** (Thinkstock), **22** (Ed Bock); © Getty Images pp. **17** (Minden Pictures/Suzi Eszterhas), **26** (Taxi/Seth Joel); © Photodisc p. **21**; © Punchstock (Digital Vision) p. **8**.

Note paper design features with permission of ©istockphoto.com.

Every effort has been made to contact copyright holders of material reproduced in this book. Any omissions will be rectified in subsequent printings if notice is given to the publishers.

Contents

What is a presentation? 4

Choosing a topic 8

Doing research 10

Organizing information.. 14

Knowing the audience 16

Writing and revising... 18

Visual aids.. 22

Practise, practise, practise... 24

The presentation 26

Planning tools 28

Research resources.. 30

Glossary... 31

Index 32

Some words are printed in bold, **like this**. You can find out what they mean by looking in the glossary.

What is a presentation?

Report planner

Step 1: Write down the project and its requirements.

Step 2: Note the due date.

Step 3: Get started right away!

Today's science lesson deals with different **endangered species**. The teacher tells the class how tigers, whales, and grey wolves became endangered in the wild. "Class," she says, "I want each of you to choose an endangered animal to study. In two weeks, you will give a presentation. Tell us how that animal became endangered and what is being done to save the species." Jess writes down the project. What animal should she study?

Understand the project

Giving a presentation makes many students nervous. However, students give presentations every day. Answering a question in class is a short presentation. Telling a friend what happened at last night's football match is also a presentation.

Understanding the project is the first step to a successful presentation. What is the subject of the presentation? How long does it need to be? When is it due? Do you need to hand in a written report or just give the presentation? Should you use a display when giving the presentation? How will you be marked? If there is any part of the project you do not understand, ask the teacher.

Your teacher can answer any questions that you might have about the presentation.

Types of presentations

Presentations, also called speeches, tell the **audience** something. There are four different jobs that they can do. A presentation can give information. It can **demonstrate** how something works. A presentation can **persuade** the audience or it can entertain them.

A speech about how an animal species became endangered informs the audience. A science experiment done for the class is a **demonstration**. Television advertisements and team talks persuade the listener. Speakers entertain audiences by telling stories or jokes.

Presentations may serve several purposes at once. For example, the main purpose of your presentation on an endangered species is to inform the audience. If you begin your presentation with an **anecdote** about an endangered animal, the presentation also entertains. If the information is interesting, you might persuade listeners to work towards helping a species survive.

Main purpose	Type of presentation	
To inform	Biographies Sports Maths principles	History News Directions
To demonstrate	Maths process How to build or make something Skills (sports, music, art)	Science experiments Cooking
To persuade	Debates Arguments Commercials or advertisements	Political speeches Book or film reviews
To entertain	Stories Poems Songs or jingles	Jokes Anecdotes

TWIST OF THE TONGUE

Tongue twisters help you develop good speaking skills.
Read this three times quickly:

Sally Shelly sells selfish shellfish.

Parts of the presentation

A presentation has three main sections: the **introduction**, the **body**, and the **conclusion**. The introduction should grab the listeners' attention. The body provides main ideas and supporting facts. The conclusion wraps up the speech.

An introduction needs to be short and catchy. In some ways, the introduction teases the audience. It grabs the listeners' attention and makes them want to hear more. Experienced speakers often use a fascinating fact, a quote, or a story as a way to introduce their topic.

HELPFUL HINT!

With a speech, listeners cannot go back and reread important material. If something is very important, repeat the information later in your speech.

The body makes up the bulk of the presentation. In a 3-minute speech, the body should take about 2 minutes while the introduction and conclusion take about 30 seconds each. This is where you present your ideas about the topic. It also contains all the facts, details, dates, and other information that supports the main ideas. The body needs to be organized in a clear way.

In the body, introduce a main idea and provide the material that supports it. Repeat key facts to help listeners understand important ideas. For example, you might tell the audience that whales became endangered because of over hunting. Give facts and figures about whale hunting. Then, remind the listeners that hunting threatens the survival of whales.

The conclusion, like the introduction, is short. Leave the audience with something to think about. Conclude the topic. Make a statement. Ask the audience to take action. Whatever you decide to use for your conclusion, do it quickly.

Make a schedule

To make sure you get your work done on time, begin by setting up a schedule that includes all of the different parts of your project. Start your project early enough to allow plenty of time to get everything finished.

Make a schedule that allows you to get the work done on time. Here is an example:

Monday	Tuesday	Wednesday	Thursday	Friday
Week 1 Choose topic Begin research	Research	Research	Research	Sort information
Monday	Tuesday	Wednesday	Thursday	Friday
Week 2 Write speech	Make note cards. Make display poster.	Practise	Practise	Give the presentation

CHAPTER CHECKLIST

✓ I know what is required.
✓ I start work immediately.
✓ I plan my work in advance.

Choosing a topic

Report planner

Step 1: Brainstorm possible topics.

Step 2: Pre-research topic options.

Step 3: Choose the topic.

Jess does not know which endangered animal to study. She reviews a list of endangered species posted on a display board, then she **brainstorms** a list of animals that interest her. She does some **pre-research** in the school library. After seeing what material is available, Jess picks mountain gorillas for her topic.

Choosing the right topic

Sometimes a teacher provides specific topics for a presentation. Other times, pupils can pick their own topics. If you have a choice, pick a subject that appeals to you. You will have more fun and do a better job if you are interested in the topic.

Be sure to consider your audience when picking a topic. For your presentation to be a success, you must keep the audience's attention. You might be interested in endangered armoured snails, but will your audience want to hear about them? You want to choose a topic that will excite the audience.

Do some pre-research to find out if there is enough available material on your topic. Look up the subject on an Internet **search engine** or on the library's **OPAC**. If there is plenty of material available, your **research** will be easier.

After brainstorming several possible topics, Jess decides to study mountain gorillas.

Expanding or narrowing a topic

A topic can be too large or too small to make a good presentation subject, so make sure your topic is neither too broad nor too narrow. It would be impossible to talk about all endangered species in a three-minute presentation. It might also be hard to come up with enough to say about one particular endangered animal.

There are many ways to expand or narrow a topic. Think about the general topic from different angles. For example, the topic is endangered species. One approach might be to research a specific species. Another idea might be to look at a family of animals. Broaden the topic from a Grecian Copper butterfly (too narrow) to endangered European butterflies (just right).

Try another approach. There are several species of endangered big cats. One way to examine the topic would be to study only tigers. Another idea might be to study all big cats suffering from **habitat** loss. A third idea might be endangered cats of Asia, such as tigers, Asian lions, snow leopards, and so on. Work on your topic until you have enough material to fill your presentation, but not too much material to cover within the time limit.

Narrow your topic to a reasonable size.

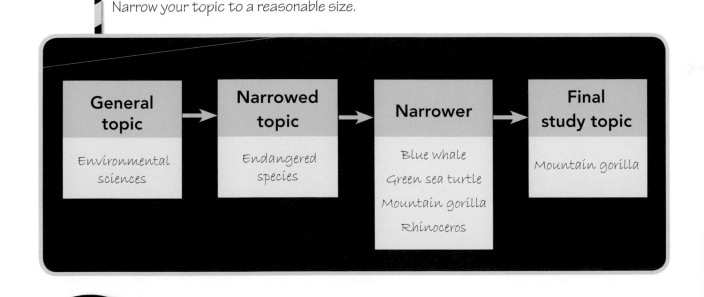

General topic	Narrowed topic	Narrower	Final study topic
Environmental sciences	Endangered species	Blue whale Green sea turtle Mountain gorilla Rhinoceros	Mountain gorilla

CHAPTER CHECKLIST

✓ I chose a topic.
✓ I viewed the topic from different angles.
✓ I adjusted the topic to a manageable size.

Doing research

Report planner

Step 1: Take a trip to the library.

Step 2: Surf the Internet.

Step 3: Ask an expert for information.

Jess uses a **planning tool** known as a KWL chart to begin her research on mountain gorillas. KWL stands for "what you Know, what you Want to know, and what you have Learned". Jess writes down what she already knows and what she wants to know. She will fill in the "Learned" box as she does her research.

Finding information

When you research a topic, begin with what you already know. Use that information to guide your research. For example, suppose your topic is tigers. You might want to look for information about tigers, endangered animals, Asian animals, and big cats.

You should look for information in several different books, magazines, or videos. These are called sources. Collect at least three to five sources to find the material you need. You will find information at both school and public libraries and on the Internet.

Use a KWL chart to begin your research.

What you KNOW	What you WANT to know	What you have LEARNED
Mountain gorillas: Endangered Live in Africa	Why endangered? What happened? Who is helping? What stands in the way of survival?	?

Using the library

Libraries are organized to make finding information easy. They have separate sections for fiction and non-fiction books, videos, audiobooks, magazines, newspapers, and **reference** materials.

Begin your research by searching OPAC. You can search by title, author, or subject. OPAC lists books, videos, DVDs, and audiotapes. The non-fiction section is organized by the **Dewey decimal system**. Every non-fiction subject has an assigned number. For instance, go to the non-fiction book area, look for 599.758, and you will find books on tigers.

Use a book's table of contents and index to pinpoint the information you are looking for. For example, the table of contents will tell you if there is a chapter specifically on tiger **conservation**. The index will list specific pages where you will find information on habitat loss or over hunting.

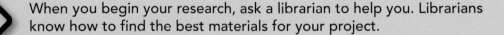

HELPFUL HINT! When you begin your research, ask a librarian to help you. Librarians know how to find the best materials for your project.

You should also look for magazine articles on your research topic. Ask the librarian to help you. You may need to access a **subscription database** through the library computer. Use this in the same way you use a search engine. Enter the topic you want researched, and the database will list articles on that topic.

You may be allowed to print out material you find on the Internet. Make sure you ask the librarian if printing is allowed and how many pages you may print. If you cannot print information from the Internet, write the important facts and the source on note cards.

Using the Internet

Many people do research on the Internet, and there is plenty of **reference** material available. The best way to find what you need is to use a search engine. A search engine finds articles and websites on a specific topic in a matter of seconds.

Control your search by defining the narrowest possible topic. Look for "blue whale conservation" rather than just "whales" or "conservation". Enter the subject in the search window, click the "go" button, and poof! You have instant research. You may get thousands of hits – sources and sites – on your topic.

There are a number of reference websites on the Internet with links to dictionaries, government websites, newspapers, and magazines. Try www.shef.ac.uk/library/useful, which has a good list of resources. The British Library also has a useful website.

Many websites will also have lists of favourite links to other websites on similar topics. Keep a note pad by the computer. Carefully write down the names or addresses of the best sites you find. That way, you can return to those sites again. If you are using your own computer, you might want to bookmark a helpful site.

You may do research at home, at school, or in the library.

HELPFUL HINT!

If you are studying a current topic, try to use books and articles published in the last five years. Those materials will have the most recent information.

Choosing appropriate information

Once the search list pops up, you must sort trusted sources from those that contain false or inaccurate information. On the Internet, look for sources that have .gov, .org, or .edu in their addresses. Government agencies run .gov websites. Org refers to organizations, such as zoos, museums, charities, or conservation groups. Edu is the address for schools, colleges, and universities. Websites and articles with these addresses usually provide more accurate information than .com sites.

Personal interviews

Experts can be excellent sources. When you ask an expert questions, the process is called an interview. How do you find an expert to interview? Suppose you are researching black rhinos. There are several organizations that are working to save black rhinos. These groups have websites on the Internet and contact information. Send an email with your questions to the organization, and you will get a response. You might also find an expert listed in an article about your subject.

Whether you do your interview in person, by phone, or by email, be prepared. Write down five questions you need answered. Make sure you say "thank you" when the interview is over.

CHAPTER CHECKLIST

✓ I used several sources.
✓ I used an Internet search engine.
✓ I used reliable resources.

Organizing information

Report planner

Step 1: Sort notes by subjects.

Step 2: Use a planning tool.

Step 3: Organize notes in a logical order.

Jess needs to get organized. She collects her notes and decides to arrange her speech according to causes and effects. She has discovered three major reasons why mountain gorillas have become endangered. Jess has also found four fascinating facts about gorillas that she will use in her speech.

Sorting and organizing information

As you do your research, take notes on index cards. These cards come in different sizes. On the top of each card, write the subject, the source, and the page number where the information was found. This will help for sorting notes later on.

Each note should be short. Just write the facts, details, dates, or other important information on the topic in your own words. If you use someone else's words, you must give that person credit for what they said. Using another author's material without giving them credit is called **plagiarism**, and it is against the law.

Every time you change the topic, use a new note card. For example, you research giant pandas. On one note card, you write about what pandas eat. You write about the loss of panda habitats on a different card.

TWIST OF THE TONGUE

Try this tongue twister:

A quick-witted cricket critic.

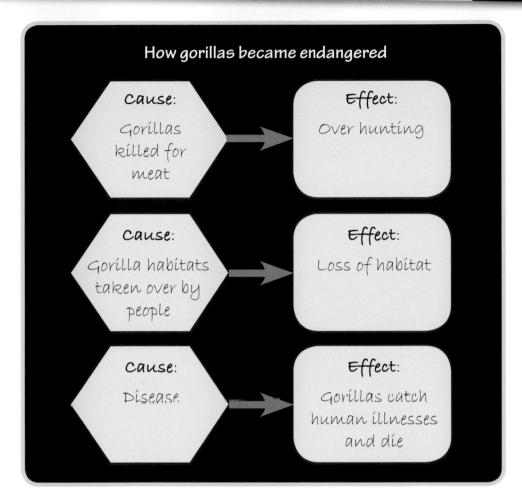

How gorillas became endangered

Cause: Gorillas killed for meat → Effect: Over hunting

Cause: Gorilla habitats taken over by people → Effect: Loss of habitat

Cause: Disease. → Effect: Gorillas catch human illnesses and die

Using planning tools

Planning tools help sort information. Different planning tools work well for different types of information. You do not need to use complete sentences in a planning tool. Just put the main ideas and facts down in short phrases.

You can find examples of useful planning tools at the end of this book or on the Internet. Use a planning tool to refine your ideas into smaller categories. Then, sort your note cards according to those categories. Put the note cards in the order in which you plan to use them and number each card. You are almost ready to write your speech.

CHAPTER CHECKLIST

✓ I made notes on index cards.
✓ I organized subject categories.
✓ I put my notes in a useful order.

Knowing the audience

Report planner

Step 1: Consider what your audience knows.

Step 2: Look for fascinating facts.

Step 3: Use repetition and concrete examples.

Jess needs to consider what her class already knows about her topic. She is sure the class knows that mountain gorillas live in Africa, but the class may not know about the countries of Uganda and Rwanda. She will add some key information about this environment to her speech.

What the audience knows

The **content** of a speech depends on the audience. For example, a presentation given to a class in school would include simpler material than a speech given to scientists. The less the audience already knows, the more you have to explain.

Your audience is made up of classmates. You will probably all share the same basic knowledge. As you plan your presentation, ask yourself some questions: What does my audience want to know? What fascinating facts might keep them interested in my presentation?

Using fascinating facts

Whenever you do research, you will discover some really interesting facts. Become a fascinating fact collector. Sprinkle these facts throughout your report, and you will find your classmates listening to what you say. These facts should fit in with the information given in your presentation.

What makes a fact fascinating? A common fact is something most people already know. A fascinating fact is something outrageous, unbelievable, weird, or interesting. A common fact is that blue whales have tongues. A fascinating fact is that their tongues are so big that a full-sized elephant could stand on one and have room left over!

For the first three months of a baby gorilla's life, its mother never puts it down – not even when she sleeps. This is an example of a fascinating fact.

HELPFUL HINT! Look up fascinating facts about your topic. If you can quickly find five or more interesting facts, you have the start for an exciting presentation.

Helping your listener

Listeners will understand your report better if you provide some help. **Repetition** is a key "helper". Repeat important facts, figures, or ideas. Change the wording when you repeat the material, but make sure you repeat main ideas and supporting facts.

The information you give should be **concrete**. In a speech, concrete information includes solid, actual facts that make a point. It is one thing to say, "Whaling killed lots of whales." It is better to say, "During the 1900s, about 360,000 blue whales were killed by hunters in the Antarctic alone."

CHAPTER CHECKLIST
- ✓ I considered my audience.
- ✓ I found fascinating facts.
- ✓ I plan to use repetition and concrete facts.

Writing and revising

Report planner

Step 1: Plan a short opening statement.

Step 2: Use an outline or planning tool for the body.

Step 3: Conclude quickly at the end.

Jess is not sure how to write a presentation, so she asks her teacher what to do. The teacher suggests that Jess write only the introduction and the conclusion. She tells Jess to use an outline or main idea chart for the body of the report. She says, "Speak from your notes instead of reading your presentation word for word."

Writing the presentation

A presentation needs to grab the audience from the first sentence. The introduction is short: three or four sentences make a good opener. Use the introduction to catch the listeners' attention and announce the topic.

There are several standard types of introductions that interest an audience. Some speakers start with a quote. The quote chosen should come from an expert or a well-known person. Another good opener is a fascinating fact. Tell the fact, and then draw the audience in by explaining how that fact connects to your topic. Another idea might be to link your presentation to others heard before. Begin with "You know what has happened to tigers and leatherback turtles. Now, I'm going to tell you what is happening with rhinos, and the news is not good."

HELPFUL HINT!

Use a highlighter to highlight key words, phrases, facts, or quotes in your presentation. This will help you find your place as you speak.

The body – outline or chart

Now you are ready to work on the body of your speech. This is the longest part – about two-thirds of the presentation. Unless your teacher asks you to hand in a written version of your presentation, the body does not need to be written out word for word. What you really need is a guide to organize your main ideas and supporting facts.

An outline is one way to arrange material in the order in which it is to be presented. Outlines have three basic parts: main ideas, sub-topics, and supporting details. Follow the sample graphic below for the general layout of an outline.

A main idea chart is another way to arrange information. Use one page or large note card for each main idea. Write the idea in a box on the left of the page or note card. List two or three supporting facts or details on the right-hand side. See a sample of a main idea chart on page 29 of this book.

Make an outline to organize your material. Here is an example:

Mountain gorillas

I. Habitat
  a. Rwanda
  b. Uganda
  c. Mountain forests

II. Reasons they are endangered
  a. Poaching or hunting
  b. Loss of habitat
  c. Disease

III. Helping gorillas
  a. Organizations
    1. International gorilla Conservation programme
    2. Conservation and research for endangered species
    3. Mountain gorilla conservation fund
  b. Dian Fossey
  c. Zoos

Writing the conclusion

A conclusion needs to be as short as the introduction. Three or four sentences are enough. Begin by restating the main idea of your presentation. Then, end the same way you began. Use a quote, a fascinating fact, or some connection to other information in your presentation. You might also use a call to action. Ask people to do something. For example, "We can help whooping cranes survive. Let's adopt a whooper through a zoo!"

Making note cards

You can give your presentation from full-sized pages, but index cards are easier to manage. Transfer your notes onto index cards. Try not to put too many words on any card. You want the notes to remind you of what to say, not record every word. Just record the important facts or phrases that will serve as **cues** as you speak.

When you use quotes, write each quote on a note card. Mark the place where the quote belongs in your outline or chart. You should give the author credit for what is said. Say something like: "According to Jane Goodall, an expert on chimpanzees…" Do not try to memorize the quote – just read it.

Number each card in order of use. If your cards get out of order, you can quickly sort them. When you have your notes in order, do your first practice speech.

Here is a sample note card:

Chimpanzees	Jane Goodall, 2006 Interview, *Sierra Magazine*	Card #5
	"Worldwide there are more human children born every day than the total number of great apes left in the wild, which is about 300,000 at the most and decreasing all the time."	

Revising the presentation

Time your speech by using a clock. Do not stop for mistakes or to reword a section. How long did the presentation take? Did it meet the assignment's requirements? If your speech runs short, you need to add more information. If it is too long, think about what can be removed without harming the presentation.

When speaking in front of a group, you will talk faster than during practice. A practice speech that takes four minutes will probably last less than three minutes in front of an audience. Keep this in mind to ensure your speech will meet the minimum time requirement.

When practising your presentation, use a clock to check that the presentation is within the time limits your teacher suggested.

CHAPTER CHECKLIST

✓ I wrote a catchy introduction and conclusion.
✓ I arranged notes for the body.
✓ I made note cards.

Visual aids

Jess's presentation is ready, but she feels that it needs some visual help. She thinks a map of eastern Africa with locations of mountain gorilla populations might help. She would also like to show pictures of mountain gorillas in their natural habitat.

Posters

Posters are usually viewed from a distance. The pictures and words need to be large. This can be hard to do. When you work on a poster, everything is close and looks the correct size. Your audience will not be so close. Test the **visibility** of your poster from at least 4.5 metres (15 feet) away.

Posters are a good way to show charts and graphs, pictures, diagrams of how something works, and illustrations. Make sure you provide a headline on your poster and readable labels of key items.

If your classroom already has a map, you might use that one instead of making your own map.

Maps

Maps are ideal for showing your audience where something took place or where something is located. Use maps in history, geography, or science reports when the place is important. Include the area and enough surrounding land to help the audience relate to the place discussed. For instance, Galapagos tortoises are only found on the Galapagos Islands, but where are they? A map of the islands is good; a map that shows the islands' distance from a known place, such as South America, is better.

Handouts

Sometimes an idea is too difficult or needs too much explanation for a poster. If so, you might think about making a handout. Handouts are good for complicated diagrams or illustrations, extensive scientific procedures, or history timelines.

Demonstrations and experiments

There is nothing that makes a science report as exciting as doing demonstration in class. Demonstrations and experiments are a good way to show an audience how to make something or how a process works. Such displays work well for science, maths, and cooking. Explain your idea completely to your teacher and ask permission to do your demonstration or experiment. You would also need to test your experiment to make sure it works, and bring all materials with you.

Models

A model is a three-dimensional display of a process, a structure of some type, a scene, or a moment in history. A **diorama** of a scene from a book or a play adds to a book presentation. Models of an explorer's ship would interest an audience, as would a model of an early telephone or a miniature bridge or castle.

CHAPTER CHECKLIST

✓ I chose useful visual aids.
✓ I made the materials early.
✓ I tested the materials from a distance.

Practise, Practise, Practise

Report planner

Step 1: Practise your report several times alone.

Step 2: Ask family or friends to be an audience.

Step 3: Use visual aids when practising.

Jess needs an audience. Her older brother has done many presentations in school, so she asks him to listen to her. She sets up her poster and map in front of the living room sofa and begins. "Mountain gorillas are nearly human. They have families, love their children, and share meals together. Sadly, their greatest threat to survival comes from one of their closest relatives – humans."

Personal practice

A good speech must be practised several times. Set up your presentation in front of a mirror and then talk to yourself. Present the presentation from beginning to end, including drawing attention to your visual aids.

On a separate note card write something like: TALK ABOUT MAP HERE. Highlight this so that you do not read it by mistake. Insert the note card in the exact place where you wish to discuss the visual aid. This will remind you to call attention to a poster, map, or graph at the right time.

Go through your complete speech, and then make notes on areas that need work. Go over the rough areas at least twice. Then, repeat the entire speech from the beginning. Keep practising until you have a smooth, easy presentation, but don't try to memorize it.

Using your voice and body

If you are nervous talking in front of a group, you need to work on your voice. Make sure you speak loudly enough to be heard from the back of the room. Practise talking slowly and clearly.

Before you begin speaking, think about your voice and your body. Stand up straight and smile. Take just a moment to collect your thoughts, breathe deeply, and begin.

A sample audience

Two days before you are due to deliver your presentation, practise in front of an audience. This practice will be a **dress rehearsal**. Ask your audience – your parents, friends, or other family members – to time your presentation for you. Once you begin, go through to the end even if you make mistakes. When you are done, ask for helpful suggestions to improve your presentation. Work on the areas that need improvement and ask your audience to listen again the next day.

CHAPTER CHECKLIST

✓ I practised my presentation.
✓ I used a strong voice.
✓ I gave my presentation to a sample audience.

The presentation

Report planner

Step 1: Handle stage fright.

Step 2: Use good presentation skills.

Step 3: Smile!

Jess brings her note cards and visual aids to school. Just before she is to give her presentation, Jess breathes slowly several times to calm her nerves. She reviews her note cards before getting up in front of the class. She is confident that she will do well. The teacher says, "Jess, are you ready?" Jess smiles.

Stage fright

The jitters you feel just before you give a speech are natural. You have stage fright. Even the most experienced actors and politicians feel butterflies in their stomachs before a big event. The best cure for stage fright is knowing your material. If you've done the work and practised, your presentation will go well.

Before you begin speaking try these three relaxation techniques: Take a few deep breaths. Then, clench your hands tightly and relax them three times. Finally, imagine yourself going through your speech calmly. See yourself as a success.

See yourself as a success – and you will be!

If you make a mistake, smile, collect your thoughts, and keep going. Don't let one tiny error take over your presentation.

Look around the audience and pick a friendly face. When you begin speaking, pretend you are only talking to that friend. As you relax, you can look around the room and make eye contact with others. Concentrate on what you are saying so that you won't be distracted.

Presentation skills

Giving a speech from note cards may seem difficult, but it is really the easiest method. Reading a presentation can become boring to the audience. Memorizing takes too much time, and you may forget something and get confused. Note cards produce the best result for you and your audience.

Make sure you speak clearly, slowly, and with **expression**. Breathe evenly, pausing when appropriate. Stand up straight and, above all, smile. Relax, you do not have to be perfect.

What did you learn?

Throughout your life, you will be called on to speak in front of many groups. You may become a teacher, a lawyer, or a doctor. You may be a sports announcer, a news reporter, or a radio chat host. You will work with other people, and you will need to explain your ideas and actions. Presentations are part of everyday life. So, take a deep breath, smile … and begin.

CHAPTER CHECKLIST

✓ I have my materials ready.
✓ I practised.
✓ I will be successful!

Planning tools

Planning tools help you sort research, understand materials, and study for tests. Choose one that fits your needs.

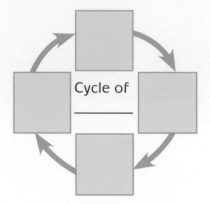

Cycle of events

Use a cycle of events chart to record a continuing process, such as the life cycle of a butterfly or the water cycle.

Chain of events

When trying to organize a sequence of events, use a chain of events chart. It is particularly good for arranging information for demonstrations or for a biography or history project.

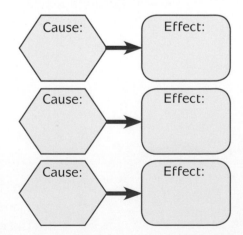

Cause and effect

A cause-and-effect chart allows you to relate events (causes) and the results (effects) of those events. A cause-and-effect chart works well for discussing scientific processes, historic events, and how or why something happened.

Idea web

An idea web helps you focus on the main idea and supporting information.

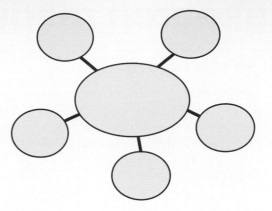

KWL (Know-Want-Learn)

Complete the "K" section of the KWL chart by providing information you already know about the topic. Determine what you want to learn and note it under "W". As you do your research, add new information under the "L" section.

What you KNOW	What you WANT to know	What you have LEARNED

Main idea

Use this chart to identify the main idea of a passage or paragraph and the information that supports the main idea.

	Supporting information:
Main idea:	Supporting information:
	Supporting information:

Research resources

In the library

Almanacs
An almanac is published every year. It contains facts, figures, and statistics on many different topics. Make sure you use the most recent edition to get current facts.

Atlases
An atlas is a book of maps, usually covering the entire world. Additional maps may show the oceans, ocean currents, agriculture, how land is used, and population.

Dictionaries
Most dictionaries do more than just give definitions of words. Standard dictionaries may contain **synonyms**, pronunciation, usage, and word origin. There are also biographical and geographical dictionaries.

Encyclopaedias
An encyclopaedia contains information on a wide variety of subjects. There are also narrower versions, such as an encyclopaedia of mammals, sports, plants, and so on.

School or public librarians
When doing research you should first talk to a librarian. Librarians know how to find information and how to get that information for you.

On the Internet

Homework help
There are many sites that offer help with homework. The BBC Schools site – www.bbc.co.uk/schools – has help on all the primary subjects.

Internet Public Library
The Internet Public Library (www.ipl.org) is like having a library on your computer. You can search through the site for information on geography, science, literature, history, and so on. You can read a book, a magazine, or a newspaper.

Online news
Most major newspapers, news magazines, and television stations have news websites. Many have search windows. Enter your topic and click "search".

Search engines
Search engines have many interesting names – Ask.com, Google, and Yahoo, to name a few. Each of these search engines works in the same way. Enter a topic in the search window, click, and the engine finds articles and websites that fill your request. Be patient. You may not find what you need on the first attempt.

Glossary

anecdote short, personal story of an incident or event

audience group of people who watch and listen to a presentation

body main section of a speech or written piece

brainstorm come up with quick ideas on a topic

conclusion end of a speech or written piece

concrete certain and specific, rather than vague or general

conservation act of saving or preserving something, such as an animal or plant species

content material or ideas in a document, book, or other source

cue something said, done, or written that reminds someone to do or say something

demonstrate show how something works

demonstration display given to others to show how something is done or how something works

Dewey decimal system system of arranging non-fiction materials by assigning numbers to specific topics

diorama three-dimensional representation of a scene, such as those seen in museums

dress rehearsal practice of something that will be presented to an audience

endangered close to extinction or no longer being in existence

expression way of communicating thoughts, feelings, or information

habitat natural conditions in which a plant or animal lives

introduction opening of a speech or written piece

OPAC (Online Public Access Catalogue) tool for finding library materials by author, title, or subject

persuade convince someone

plagiarism use someone else's written ideas without giving them credit for the material

planning tool visual aid for sorting information

pre-research look into a topic before beginning the actual project

reference source of information

repetition process of saying or writing something again

research look up information about a subject

search engine program on the Internet designed to find articles and websites on specific topics

species basic biological classification of an animal or plant

subscription database collection of magazine articles, documents, quotes, or pictures

synonym word with the same or similar meaning, such as "home" and "house"

visibility being able to be clearly seen

Index

audience 5, 6, 7, 8, 16, 17, 18, 22, 23, 24, 25, 27

body 6, 18, 19, 21, 24
brainstorm(s) 8,

call to action 20
conclusion 6, 7, 18, 20
content 16
cue(s) 20

demonstrate, demonstration(s) 5, 23, 28
details 6, 14, 19
Dewey decimal system 11
display 4, 7
dress rehearsal 25

entertain 5
experiments 23

fact(s) 6, 8, 14, 15, 16, 17, 18, 19, 20, 30
fiction 11

handouts 23

index 11
inform(s) 5
Internet 8, 10, 12, 13, 15, 30
interview 13
introduction 6, 7, 18, 20

library, libraries 8, 10, 11, 12, 30

main idea(s) 6, 17, 19, 20, 29
main idea chart 18, 19
map(s) 22, 23, 24, 30
model(s) 23

non-fiction 11
note(s) 7, 12, 14, 15, 18, 20, 21, 24, 26, 27

OPAC 8, 11
outline 18, 19, 20

persuade 5
plagiarism 14
planning tool(s) 10, 14, 15, 18, 28
practice 7, 20, 24, 25
pre-research 8
presentation(s) 5, 24, 26

quote(s) 6, 18, 20

reference 11, 12
repetition 16, 17
research 7, 8, 10, 11, 12, 14, 16, 28
revising 18, 21

schedule 7
search engine(s) 8, 12, 13, 30
source(s) 10, 13, 14
speech(es) 5, 6, 7, 14, 15, 19, 20, 21, 24, 26, 27
subject(s) 4, 8, 9, 14, 30

table of contents 11
topic(s) 7, 8, 9, 10, 11, 12, 13, 14, 18, 30

visual aid(s) 22, 23, 26
voice 24, 25

website(s) 12, 13, 30
written report 4